An Early Oklahoma Coloring Book
by
Jerald Pope

My grandmother, Ruby Graves, was born in Indian Territory. Her grandfather was a horse-and-buggy doctor in the (to be) Oklahoma City area. My mom and dad grew up in Tulsa during the Depression. I was born in Stillwater while dad was on the GI bill at OSU. So I'm about as native an Okie as you can be without actually being a Native Oklahoman.

When I look at the history of Oklahoma, it's a hard story. While that's certainly true of every state in the Union, our particular litany of murder, deceit, betrayal, broken promises, heartbreak, and bad weather is our own. When you remove the mantle of Manifest Destiny, the conquering of the West was a bad business.

That said, this is where we are now.

My Native American friends had a very pragmatic approach to the situation. The logical choice if they wanted to survive as a conquered people. So we can learn something from that. A clear-eyed look at our history, without the jingoism, gives us a firm place to stand to start building the sort of inculsive, caring, robust state we can all be proud to call home. Black, White, Red, and Brown working together.

Maybe this coloring book can help nudge us along that path.

"The origin or genesis of states is usually obscure and legendary, with prehistoric periods from which they gradually emerge like coral islands from the deep. Shadowy and crepuscular intervals precede the day in whose uncertain light men and events, distorted or exaggerated by tradition, become fabulous like the gods and goddesses, the wars of heroes of antiquity."
John James Ingalls, 1892
quoted in *Prairie Eryth* by William Least Heat-Moon

An Early Oklahoma Coloring Book
Copyright © Jerald Pope 2016
All right reserved
ISBN: 978-0-9975582-1-0

For a FREE 20 page chronology of Oklahoma full of interesting facts,
email: oklahoma@harebrandideas.com

For information about discount copies of this book for educational purposes,
call: 828 686-3922

Resources

Baird, W. David, Danney Goble. *The Story of Oklahoma.* Norman: University of Oklahoma Press, 2007.

Leonard, Jonathan Norton, the Editors of TIME-LIFE BOOKS. *Ancient America.* Alexandria, VA: TIME-LIFE BOOKS, 1967.

McReynolds, Edwin C., Alice Marriott, Estelle Faulconer. *Oklahoma: The Story of its Past and Present.* Norman: University of Oklahoma Press, 1967.

Stuart, George E., Gene S. Stuart. *Discovering Man's Past in the Americas.* National Geographic Society, 1969.

Research: Robert Odle

Thanks to: Rilla Askew, David Billstrom, David Bizarro, Teresa Luckman, Francine Ringold, Larry Silvey

Want to know even more about Oklahoma history?
Write for a FREE 20 page Oklahoma Chronological History.
Send your email address to <oklahoma@harebrandideas.com>

For millions of years the area that would become Oklahoma was covered by a shallow ocean.

Then about 190 million years ago, the land on the East and West began to rise, leaving the ocean over the center of Oklahoma.

The sea was alive with life, like trilobites. The sandy beaches led to great Jurassic forests. Eventually, about 70 million years ago, the center rose from the ocean.

The first people in Oklahoma were the Clovis people, who lived here around 11,000 years ago. You can still find their arrow and spear heads.

About 1,000 years ago the great Mississippian Culture of mound builders spread as far west as Eastern Oklahoma. The Caddoans built the great Spiro Mounds in Oklahoma.

Around 1300 years ago the Witchita Plains Culture occupied western Oklahoma. By their villages they grew corn, beans, squash, marsh elder, and tobacco. They hunted deer, turkey, and bison and fished the rivers.

The Kiowa moved into the fertile plains areas along the Arkansas River. They eventually ranged from Montana down into Texas.

In 1541 Francisco Vásquez de Coronado led an expedition northward across the Oklahoma panhandle in search of cities of gold. He returned to Mexico after failing to find them in Kansas.

In 1719 Jean-Baptiste Bérnard led an expedition from the Red River through eastern Oklahoma to explore trade possibilities with the inhabitants. Several more trips led to trade with the Witchitas and Osage.

By 1800 the Osage had established villages in the Three Forks area, driving the Witchitas away. In 1802 two French brothers, Pierre and Auguste Chouteau established a trading post.

After the Louisiana Purchase in 1803, President Jefferson sent Captain Richard Sparks to explore the Red River. They barely got to Oklahoma when Spanish cavalry (tipped off by an American general who hoped to start a war with Spain) overran their camp and forced them to turn back.

Jefferson wanted Louisiana to let those tribes who did not want to adapt to new ways move west. At his urging many Delaware, Shawnee, Choctaw, and Cherokees moved west of the Mississippi River. By 1817 nearly one-third of the Cherokees lived west of the Mississippi.

Fort Smith and Fort Gibson were built to prevent inter-tribal warfare. In 1819 English botanist Thomas Nutall joined Major William Bradford at Fort Smith for an expedition to the Red River where they found 200 white families squatting near the Poteau River. Major Bradford evicted them from their farms.

Rivers were major routes for white people. After 1820, keel boats were the primary water transport.

By 1830 only about 6,000 of the Five Tribes had moved to Oklahoma. President Andrew Jackson persuaded Congress to pass the Indian Removal Act, which forced the Five "Civilized" Tribes to leave their traditional lands to White settlers. Over 11,000 Choctaws travelled by foot, horse, and wagon to the Mississippi where they boarded boats for the Arkansas, Ouchita, and Red Rivers. They were promised they would never be included in any state or territory.

One of the boats carrying the Creeks to Oklahoma sank with 311 passengers aboard. About 3,000 Creeks died during the removal.

The last to be removed were the Cherokees. They suffered cold, hunger, disease and harassment by whites as they travelled west. About 1,400 of the 13,000 died on the trip, which came to be called "the trail of tears." The greatest loss of life occurred the year after they arrived in Oklahoma as they struggled to adapt to their new home.

Boundaries between tribes were unclear. The Plains Indians did not like having thousands of immigrants moving onto their traditional lands. In 1832 President Jackson sent a commission to settle disputes. The Osage refused to move north to Kansas. In the middle of negotiations they casually packed their belongings and headed west to hunt buffalo.

As they went west, the Osage attacked a Wichita village. President Jackson's commission purchased a captive Kiowa girl and Wichita boy in order to return them to their tribes. The three tribes were impressed with the act and promised to come to Fort Smith to negotiate treaties.

When 11,000 Cherokees arrived in Oklahoma in 1839 they were meet by 5,000 fellow Cherokees who had already settled there. The newcomers refused to join the existing government and invoked the law of Blood Revenge. Sequoyah, a tribal leader who later developed the Cherokee alphabet, led an attempt to unify the feuding factions. Finally in 1840 they adopted a constitution set Tahlequah as their capitol.

Once the Five Tribes were settled in Oklahoma, they began to rebuild their economies. They cleared land and planted corn, beans, potatoes, peas, pumpkins, melons, and fruit trees. They established farms along the rivers where steamboats picked up produce to ship to New Orleans and other eastern cities.

In 1859 the Butterfield Overland Mail established a road through Oklahoma, connecting St. Louis with California. There were fourteen stations in the Choctaw Nation to change horses.

Missionaries had been active among Native Americans long before the removals. Some were already in Oklahoma, some came with the eastern tribes. Many Native American converted to Christianity, while many stayed with their traditional religion.

The United States established more forts in the 1830s and 40s to keep peace among the tribes. The Five Tribes established inter-tribal councils to work together, with western tribes joining them.

In 1861, Confederate president Jefferson Davis sent negotiators to enlist the Native Americans, many of whom owned slaves, to the Southern cause. White abolitionist missionaries were forced to flee the territory.

About 7,000 Creeks and Seminoles, loyal to the United States, battled a group of 1,400 Native American and members of the 4th Texas cavalry near Round Mountain, east of Stillwater. The Confederates lost 10 men, while the Unionist lost 110, and were forced to retreat to Kansas.

General Stand Waite and the First Indian Brigade waged guerrilla raids on Union steamboats and supply lines. He was the last Confederate general to surrender.

The U.S. government said, since some had sided with the rebels, the members of the Five Tribes had forfeited their lands (though many had fought for the Union). The tribes had to abolish slavery and give their former slaves land and citizenship. The former slaves of Indians were some of the few who actually recieved "forty acres and a mule." This led, within a few generations, to the rise of a vibrant Black middle class in Oklahoma.

The Five Tribes had to cede all their western land to the federal government, which assigned it to Plains Indians. A new Removal Act forced 25 small tribes to move to Indian Territory. Part of the land was never assigned and non-Indians began pressuring the government to open it to white settlement.

Some of the tribes expanded their ranching efforts. Several cattle trails crossed Oklahoma from Texas to the Kansas railheads. Contrary to popular myth, most cowboys were former slaves, Mexicans, or Native Americans.

Tribal leaders began to see their former slaves as disruptive and sent vigilantes to execute or whip trouble makers. For safety, African-Americans settled near one another in all-Black communities like Redbird.

After the Civil War many white outlaws sought refuge in Indian Territory. These included the James brothers, the Younger gang, the Dalton brothers, and Belle Starr.

Many of the Plains Indians did not want to give up their traditional ways and left the reservations to follow the buffalo. On November 27, 1868, Colonel George Custer led the Seventh Cavalry in an attack on a Cheyenne camp on the Washita River. 100 Cheyenne were killed, including old people, women, and children as well as 800 horses. The cavalry lost 30 men.

The Missouri, Kansas, and Texas Railroad was the first to cross Indian Territory in 1872. It was followed by the St. Louis and San Francisco Railroad, the Atchison, Topeka and Santa Fe, Rock Island, and others.

To combat the outlaws hiding there, the government gave jurisdiction over Indian Territory to the Western District court of Arkansas in Fort Smith. In 1875 Isaac Parker "the hanging judge," took the bench there. He gathered a group of tough U.S. marshalls, including Bill Tighman, who was white, and Bass Reeves, who was black.

Congress passed the Dawes Act in 1887 which divided the land previously held in common by the tribes into privately owned parcels of 160 acres. Land left over after the division became U.S. public land, subject to the Homestead Act.

President Benjamin Harrison set high noon on April 22, 1889, for the land run that would allow white settlers to claim their 160 acre homestead. Anyone in the area before that time would not be allowed to claim land. But some people hid inside the area and staked claims before the law-abiding settlers arrived; they were called "Sooners."

Thousands of people lined up for the run. By nightfall Oklahoma City, Guthrie, and other towns had been laid out and populated. Guthrie had a population of between 12,000 and 20,000 on the first day. Initially people lived in tents, but lumber was soon being shipped in by rail.

In 1905, the discovery of oil on the farm of Ida Glenn, south of Tulsa, started the great Oklahoma oil boom.

On November 16, 1907, President Theodore Roosevelt signed the proclaimation giving Oklahoma statehood. On the steps of the territorial capitol in Guthrie, a man dressed as a cowboy and a woman dressed as an Indian were symbolically wed, representing the joining of the two territories into one state.

Homesteaders from the more moderate East were unpleasantly surprised by the extremes of the prairie weather.

White resentment of Tulsa's prosperous African-American commercial district, known as "the Black Wall Street" led to racial tensions which boiled over on May 31, 1921. A crowd of white men, intent on lynching a black man accused of rape, met a crowd of African-Americans intent on protecting him. Yelling led to shooting, and soon white rioters were burning and looting the African-American community. It was the biggest race riot in U.S. history.

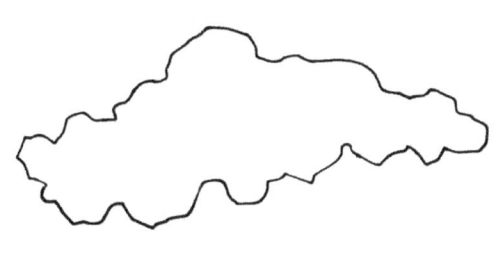

The Oklahoma Socialist Party joined with the Democrats in 1922 to elect one of their members, John Calloway Walton, governor. Governor Walton soon came in conflict with the Ku Klux Klan, which was very active nationwide, and particularly in Oklahoma. In 1923, with Klan support, Walton was impeached and removed from office.

The growth of the oil industry in the Teens and Twenties led to the growth of oil fortunes in Oklahoma. Tulsa became the "Oil Capitol of the World" and the home of many fabulous "oil mansions." In the Twenties, oil wealth and Art Deco architects combined to make Tulsa a modernist dream. Boston Avenue Methodist Church is the crowning glory of the Art Deco movement.

Will Rogers was born, November 4, 1879, on his family's farm near Oolagah, Indian Territory. As a young man he worked on the 101 Ranch, home of the internationally touring 101 Ranch's Wild West Show. Starting as a trick roper, Rogers joined the Ziegfeld Follies in New York where his wry, folksy humor led him to a successful career as a newspaper columnist and a movie star.

Stock market speculation and laissez-faire government practices create a financial bubble which burst on October 29, 1929, "Black Tuesday." The government did nothing to address the problem for three years as bank after bank closed, and depositors lost all their savings. Farmers, who often depended on credit between crops, were particularly hard hit.

From 1931 to 1939 drought brought another disaster to Oklahoma - the Dust Bowl. Huge clouds of fine dust would cover the land like black snow. People who hadn't already lost everything to the Depression gave up trying to grow anything, abandoned their farms, and migrated west to California. Whether they were from Kansas, Texas, or other afflicted states, these migrants were called "Okies."

Woody Guthrie, born in Okemah, Oklahoma, learned music busking around Oklahoma and Texas. During the Depression, he joined the Okies in California where his sympathy for the plight of the common man led to his writing some of America's most loved songs, including "This Land is Your Land."

Though many state legislators were opposed to accepting help from the federal government, The CCC (Civilian Conservation Corp) through the WPA (Works Progress Administration) employed thousands of Oklahomans to build roads, bridges, dams, parks, campgrounds, and other public works.

With the advent of World War Two in 1941, factories and businesses sprung up in Tulsa, Oklahoma City, and other cities to make ammunition, airplanes, and other war materiel. Oklahoma and the nation put the Depression behind them and set about winning the war.